6/21
water damage

Triceratops

BY BARBARA ALPERT

Amicus High Interest is published by Amicus
P.O. Box 1329, Mankato, MN 56002
www.amicuspublishing.us

Library of Congress Cataloging-in-Publication Data
Alpert, Barbara.
 Triceratops / by Barbara Alpert.
     p. cm. -- (Digging for dinosaurs)
 Summary: "Describes how the Triceratops was discovered,
how paleontologists study its bones, and what the fossil
evidence tells us about the behavior of this three-horned plant-
eating dinosaur"-- Provided by publisher.
 Audience: K to grade 3.
 Includes bibliographical references and index.
 ISBN 978-1-60753-368-9 (library binding) -- ISBN 978-1-
60753-416-7 (ebook)
 1. Triceratops--Juvenile literature. I. Title.
 QE862.O65A39 2014
 567.915'8--dc23
                              2013001231

Editor   Rebecca Glaser
Series Designer   Kathleen Petelinsek
Page production   Red Line Editorial, Inc.

Photo Credits
Dreamstime, cover; Corey Ford/Stocktrek Images/Getty
Images, 5; Hemera Technologies/Thinkstock, 6; Library
of Congress, 9, 17; Popular Science Monthly Volume 67,
10; Ambient Images Inc./SuperStock Images, 13; Sergey
Krasovskiy/Stocktrek Images/Getty Images, 14; Biosphoto/
SuperStock, 18; David Grubbs/Billings Gazette/AP Images,
21; Jacques Demarthon/AFP/Getty Images, 22; DEA Picture
Library/Getty Images, 25; Stocktrek Images/SuperStock, 26;
Wolfgang Kaehler/SuperStock, 29

Printed in the United States of America at Corporate Graphics
in North Mankato, Minnesota.
7-2014 / P.O. 1226
10 9 8 7 6 5 4 3

Table of Contents

What is a Triceratops?

Triceratops looked across the pond. Was it safe? There was no T. rex around. Time to eat! The big dinosaur lowered its head. At 10 feet (3 m) tall and 30 feet (9 m) long, it was almost as big as a bus. It grabbed leaves with its parrot-like beak. Its rows of teeth chewed them up.

Huge Triceratops wade through water to find plants to eat.

5

No one knows why Triceratops
had a frill on the back of its neck.

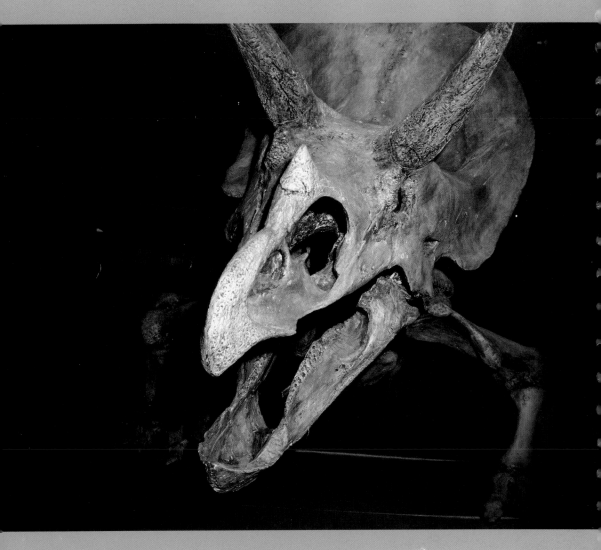

 Q How big were Triceratops' horns?

Triceratops had a powerful body. It had three sharp horns on its head. They made good **weapons**. A large, curved bone called a **frill** made it look fierce. No one knows what the frill did. Maybe it helped the dinosaur stay cool. Maybe it protected its neck. Some people think it helped them attract a mate.

The two horns on the forehead were 3 feet (0.9 m) long. **Fossils** show only the horn core. The horns were longer in real life.

The Discovery of Triceratops

The first Triceratops fossils were two horns found in 1887. They were sent to a **paleontologist** named O.C. Marsh. He thought they were buffalo horns.

In 1888, John Bell Hatcher found a large skull. He sent it to Marsh. The skull had three holes for horns. It was a new dinosaur! Marsh named it Triceratops.

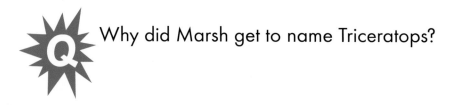 Why did Marsh get to name Triceratops?

O.C. Marsh worked at
a museum at Yale.

A He was the first to discover it.

Hatcher went back to Wyoming. During the next four years, he found 50 more Triceratops bones. He found mostly skulls. Why? Its skulls are big and heavy. They don't break or wash away as easily as smaller bones.

But what did Triceratops look like? To find out, museum workers put bones from ten Triceratops together. It was put on display in 1905.

John Bell Hatcher found 50 Triceratops bones in Wyoming.

Triceratops was a North American dinosaur. Fossils show us that it lived in Montana, Wyoming, and the Dakotas. It also lived in Canada.

Scientists have dug up leg bones of Triceratops. They have lots of ribs. But most of the bones found are skulls, horns, and parts of **skeletons**. No one has found a complete skeleton yet.

The name Triceratops means "three-horned face."

Scientists think Tyrannosaurus rex ate Triceratops.

Fossil Clues to Study

Tyrannosaurus rex likely ate Triceratops for dinner. Scientists think this for two reasons. First, they found bite marks on Triceratops fossils. The marks matched the teeth of T. rex. And in Canada, a T. rex **coprolite** was found. This is a fossil of poop. It shows what an animal ate. This one had Triceratops bone pieces in it.

In 1997, a fossil hunter dug up rare fossils. It was a baby Triceratops! It was one year old when it died. Its horns were the size of a finger. Getting the tiny bones out was hard. In 2006, another baby Triceratops was found in Montana. Baby dinosaur bones give us clues to how they grew.

 How did they get the tiny fossils out?

The horns of a baby Triceratops were about the size of a finger.

 They hammered off big rock pieces. Then they used drills like dentists use on teeth.

People create sculptures to show how the Triceratops skull looked.

Q Why did scientists say "at least three"?

Most Triceratops have been found alone. Many scientists think the dinosaur lived by itself. But in 2005, a new fossil bed was found in Montana. There were bones of at least three young Triceratops. They all died in a flood. Maybe young Triceratops did live in groups. Then they could protect each other.

 The bones were all mixed up. It will take years to dig them out. It will take even longer to know how many Triceratops died there.

How old was Triceratops? In 2011, a new Triceratops horn was found. It was in rock that some scientists think was 65 million years old. Scientists think this is when a **meteor** crashed into Earth. It wiped out all the dinosaurs. Some people disagree. They think the dinosaurs died out over many years. But Triceratops was one of the last to die.

This man found a Triceratops horn in Montana.

Piecing together dinosaur bones can be tricky.

A Digital Dinosaur

In 1999, the Triceratops at the
Smithsonian needed cleaning. Scientists
took it apart. They took a **digital** picture
of every bone. They saw how each one fit.
From the pictures, they made a **3-D** digital
model of the dinosaur. They studied how
it moved. Workers cleaned all the bones.
Then they covered them with glue so
none would crack.

The scientists also fixed mistakes. The foot bones were not from a Triceratops at all! They were from a Hadrosaur. And many of the bones were the wrong size. The scientists studied other Triceratops bones. They made **casts** of bones. Now they were the right size. The Triceratops went back on display in 2001.

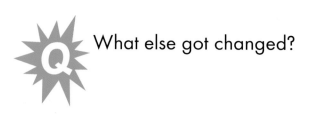 What else got changed?

Hadrosaurs were large, duck-billed dinosaurs.

 They made a bigger skull. The old one was found in pieces. But based on Triceratops fossils found later, the old one was too small.

All dinosaurs in the Ceratopsid family had horns.

Recent Finds

All horned dinosaurs belong to one family. It is called **Ceratopsids**. Many are like Triceratops. Some are a bit different. In 2010, two new horned dinosaurs were found in Utah. One had a very long skull. The other had 15 horns. Five were on its face. Ten ran across the top of its bony frill.

In August 2012, a man was walking in Alberta, Canada. He spotted large bones on a hill! He called the Royal Tyrrell Museum. They sent a team of paleontologists. They have found a Triceratops skull, backbones, and ribs. The ribs are more than 6 feet (2 m) long! The bones are being prepared for display.

A scientist works to dig up Triceratops bones in Canada.

Glossary

3-D Three dimensional, showing length, width, and height.

cast A plastic copy of a real fossil.

Ceratopsids The family name for horned dinosaurs.

coprolite A fossil of dinosaur droppings.

digital Made using a computer.

fossil The remains of a plant or animal of a past age preserved in earth or rock.

frill A fan-shaped bone on a dinosaur's neck.

meteor A piece of rock from space that falls to earth at a high speed.

paleontologist A scientist who studies fossils.

skeleton The frame of bones supporting a body.

weapon Something used in a fight.

Read More

Dodson, Peter. *Triceratops Up Close: Horned Dinosaur.* Zoom in on Dinosaurs! Berkeley Heights, N.J.: Enslow Publishers, 2011.

Mara, Wil. *Triceratops.* Rookie Read-About Dinosaurs. New York: Children's Press, 2012.

Staunton, Joseph. *Plant-Eating Dinosaurs.* Discover the Dinosaurs. Mankato, Minn.: Amicus, 2011.

Websites

Triceratops – Enchanted Learning
http://www.enchantedlearning.com/subjects/dinosaurs/dinos/Triceratops.htm

Triceratops Horridus – National Geographic Kids
http://kids.nationalgeographic.com/kids/animals/creaturefeature/triceratops-horridus/

Triceratops – theDinosaurs.org – Everything Kids Need to Know about Dinosaurs!
http://www.thedinosaurs.org/dinosaurs/triceratops.aspx

Index

About the Author

Barbara Alpert has written more than 20 children's books and many books for adults. She lives in New York City, where she works as an editor. She loves to travel and has collected fossils in New York, New Jersey, Montana, and Pennsylvania.